GREENWICH TRADITIONAL MUSICIANS CO-OPERATIVE TUNE BOOK 2008

WWW.GREENTRAD.ORG.UK

GREENWICH TRADITIONAL MUSICIANS CO-OPERATIVE TUNE BOOK

MUSIC PLAYED AT THE CRICKETERS AND LORD HOOD PUBS IN GREENWICH, LONDON, EVERY TUESDAY, C.1996-2008

Musicians' who play or have played in the session. We have not been able to remember everybody.

Andy Lamb, Alec Gorham, Sarah Crofts, Doug Adams, Paul Gross, Pete Gibson, Richard Jones, Belinda Jones, Chris Dyer, Mick Keen, Mick Malloy, Martin Brown, Gary Holden, Richard Partridge, Caroline Shaw, Verity Sharp, Bill Dudley, Dave Wright, Greg Robbins, Mick the Pole, Matt Norman, Neil Parker, Vicky Parker, Robert Watkins, Seb Morris, Tony Barron, Trevor Bennett, Tony Black, Will Summers, Will Pearce-Smith, Jack Chiswick, Dave Danford, Graham Shelver, Phil Lanzon, Susan Bell, Nic Hurst, Steve Brett, Lisa Bradley, and me, John Offord

DRAWINGS
Drawings on pages 4, 22, 43 and 65 are copyright to Paul Gross, the same as mentioned above and may not be reproduced under the same terms as below without his permission and the agreement of the secretary of the Greenwich Musicians' Co-operative.

COPYRIGHT OF TUNES
Permission to publish has been granted to Greenwich Musicians' Co-operative from all composers of tunes marked copyright

PUBLISHED IN 2008
BY GREENWICH TRADITIONAL MUSICIANS CO-OPERATIVE
All rights reserved. The text and music of this publication may not be reproduced, stored in a retrieval system or transmitted, in any form or by any means (electronic, mechanical, photocopying or otherwise), without written consent of the secretary of Greenwich Traditional Musicians' Co-operative

ISBN 978-0-9558490-0-8
(second edition April 2008)

THE MUSIC AND STRUCTURE OF THE SESSION

From 9pm to 11pm, the session is essentially of English music, although we do play some Irish and Scottish tunes. If you want to play just Irish music, go to an Irish session. You may think that what we are playing actually is just Irish music, but it is very difficult sometimes to be certain of the origin of a tune, especially jigs and hornpipes. Irish music is generally played differently and the repertoire will not resemble ours very much. Our session has been going for about 12 years, and the total number of tunes played must be nearly 250. In that time musicians' have come and gone and we have tried to remember all the tunes they played as well as our own. Some of the musicians' who come are figures from television, radio or the stage, but we welcome anyone who is competent, or wants to improve and introduce new English tunes not in this book, but bear in mind that if you are going to play hackneyed material like morris dance tunes all night, this might not be well received. After 11pm, in drinking up time, anything goes, shanties, music hall, Irish tunes etc.

THE REPRODUCTION OF THE MUSIC AND THE SOURCES

We play mainly sets of tunes. This is complicated by the fact that the order and composition of some sets has changed, so it can get even more complicated if this is changed again. Some musicians' who come are quite basic and cannot adapt quickly. We try to cater for everyone *and* introduce new tunes, for some of us have been playing for years and have access to an enormous amount of music. I have tried to reproduce all the music we play or have played in sequence from page to page, so it can be read without turning the page. Some sets of tunes have been over-played, so we try not to do them now, in spite of the fact that some of this music is rarely heard anywhere else. Some of the tunes we play are still copyrighted, so we cannot re-produce them in this book without the lengthy procedure of obtaining permission. I have tried to contact some of the composers, but I have received no replies.

There are inconsistencies in the reproduction of the music. Sometimes I have not been able to obtain the original sequence of some tunes, because the player has not been able to remember and there are limits with the software, making it very awkward to go back to adjust things like this.

The final bar in many tunes has been written as if it were leading into another tune even if it is the last tune in a set or the next tune does not have a lead-in bar. This is common practice amongst 'folkies' and so does not lead to any problems. Some tunes are written to be played with a structure like AA BA, but this is not strictly adhered to in a session. Many folk musicians' do not read music; many classical musicians' cannot play without it. It is best to be able to memorise tunes from hearing *and* written music. The advantage of the first is that a style of playing is understood, the advantage of the second is that the same old tunes are not banged out *ad nauseum*. There are definite styles of playing, for instance, fiddle music, and with the use of technology, bowings in old recordings of English as well as Irish music can now be seen. In England there are about eight thousand tunes in manuscripts, old books or from field recordings. Much of this has been found quite recently and many tune books have been published in the past 20 years containing unknown English tunes, so perhaps you would like to look at these, if not tunes in this book.

John Offord
www.johnofthegreen.co.uk

GTMC TUNE INDEX
Titles in *italics* are alternative names

A
ALDERMAN'S HAT-20
ASHLEY'S HORNPIPE- 40
ASHLEY'S RIDE-19
ATHOLE HIGHLANDER-68

B
BABES IN THE WOOD-19
BACUP COCONUT DANCE-34
BALL'S HORNPIPE-7
BARNACLE WALTZ-31
BEAR DANCE-21
BEWICKS HORNPIPE-4
BILL HALL'S NUMBER 1-18
BILL HALL'S NUMBER 2-18
BLACK JOAK-14
BLACK MARYS HORNPIPE-29
BLUE EYED STRANGER-58
BODMIN RIDING MARCH-7
BONNY BREAST KNOT-34
BONNY KATE-20
BOURREE XXX11-1
BRIGHTON CAMP-18
BROMSBERROW HEATH-42
BUTCHER'S HORNPIPE-6
BUTTERED PEAS-54

C
CAPTAIN LENOE'S QUICK MARCH-12
CHESHIRE ROUNDS-64
CHURCH STREET-61
COCK O' THE NORTH-17
COKEY HORNPIPE-2
COLEFORD JIG-38
COLLEGE HORNPIPE-3
CONSTANT BILLY-14
CRICKETERS-51
CUTTY SARK-28

D
DARK GIRL DRESSED IN BLUE-51
DASHING WHITE SERGEANT-50
DERBY KELLY-8
DEVIL AMONGST THE TAILORS-50
DORSET 4 HAND REEL-54
DORSETSHIRE HORNPIPE-36
DOUBLE LEAD THROUGH-35
DOWN WITH THE FRENCH-12
DRAPERS MAGGOT-26
DRESSED SHIP-21
DRIBBLES OF BRANDY-13
DUNMOE GALLUMPH-13
DURHAM RANGERS-45
DUSTY MILLER-27

E
EARLY ONE MORNING-2
ENGLAND'S GLORY-48
ENRICO-46

F
FAMILY JIG-9
FIELDTOWN PROCESSIONAL-62
FIERY CLOCK FACE-67
FLAT CAP-64
FLIGHT-15
FLOWERS OF EDINBURGH-51
FOX AND GEESE-8
FRED PIGEON'S NO.1-32
FRED PIGEON'S NO.2-32
FRED PIGEON'S NO.3-32
FRENCH ASSEMBLY-29

G
GALLOPEDE-5
GETTING UPSTAIRS-61
GILDEROY-22
GIRL WITH THE BLUE DRESS ON-33
GLORISHEARS-62
GLOUCESTER HORNPIPE-43
GO TO THE DEVIL-8
GREENSLEEVES-12
GREEN MOUNTAIN PETRONELLA-55
GYPSEY'S HORNPIPE-36
GYPSY HORNPIPE-44

H
HALF HANNIKIN-25
HANDSOM PLOUGHBOY-47
HARPER'S FROLICK-20
HEEL & TOE POLKA-57
HIGHLAND MARY-63
HOD THE LASS-1
HOLE IN THE WALL-25
HOP BREAK-11
HORNPIPE-28
HORNPIPE- 59
HORNPIPE-60
HORNPIPE-60
HOT PUNCH-16
HUNT THE SQUIRREL-10

HUNTSMAN'S CHORUS-53
I
INSRUCTABLE TERRIER OF BELSTONE-37
IRON LEGS-5
J
JACK ROBINSON-48
JACKS GONE A-SHEARING-27
JACKY TAR-22
JENNY LIND POLKA-33
JIG OF SLURS-68
JOCKEY SAID TO JENNY-27
JOCKEY TO THE FAIR-14
JOHN LOCKE'S HORNPIPE-42
K
KAFOOLZALUM-43
KEEL ROW-43
KETTLE DRUM-23
KEYS TO THE CELLAR-27
L
LA MAISON DE LA REINE-39
LA RUSSE-35
LEMMY BRAZIL'S NO.2-3
LET ME IN THIS NIGHT LOVE-19
LILLI BURLERO-65
LONDON HORNPIPE-37
LONDON PRIDE-63
LORD NELSON'S HORNPIPE-38
LORD NELSON'S HORNPIPE 2-60
M
MAJOR MALLEY'S REEL-21
MANCHESTER HORNPIPE-38
MAN IN THE MOON-30
MARFULL HORNPIPE-59
MERRY BELLS POLKA-56
MICHAEL TURNER'S WALTZ-29
MILL-FIELD-25
MONCK'S MARCH-62
MOLL IN THE WAD-13
MOREPETH RANT-4
MOUNTHILL'S-40
MRS GEORGE DEARINGS WALTZ-30
N
NAPOLEON'S GRAND MARCH-52
NEWCASTLE-23
NEW RIGGED SHIP-66
NO TIME FOR TEA-1

O
OATS AND BEANS-66
OFF TO CALIFORNIA-45
OLD JOE, THE BOAT IS GOING OVER (1)-58
OLD JOE, THE BOAT IS GOING OVER (2)-58
OLD LANCASHIRE HP-65
OLD MOLE-24
ONCE I LOVED A MAIDEN FAIR-25
ORANGE IN BLOOM-30
OUT IN THE OCEAN-69
OVER THE HILLS-28
P
PANTALOON QUADRILLE-9
PARSON'S FAREWELL-23
PETTICOAT LOOSE-69
PICKING OF STICKS-24
PIGEON ON THE GATE-38
PLANE TREE-11
POLLY PUT THE KETTLE ON-48
POOR ROBIN'S MAGGOT-10
PRINCESS ROYAL-63
PUNCHENELLO'S HORNPIPE-27
Q
QUAKER-61
QUEEN'S HOUSE-28
QUICKSTEP AT THE BATTLE OF PRAGUE-55
R
RADSTOCK JIG-50
RAKES OF MALLOW-57
RATHWELL HORNPIPE-28
RECOVERY-56
REDESDALE HORNPIPE-41
REDOWA POLKA-56
RICHARD'S HORNPIPE-59
RICKETTS HORNPIPE-38
RIG-A-JIG-66
ROGUE'S MARCH-17
ROSE POLKA-56
ROSE TREE-53
ROWLING HORNPIPE-29
ROXBURGH CASTLE-49
RUSSIAN WALTZ-31
S
SADLERS WELLS HORNPIPE-7
SAILORS HORNPIPE-44
SALMON TAILS-57

SCAN TESTERS SCHOTTISCHE-48
SCHOTTISCHE HORNPIPE-37
SEARCHING FOR SOAP-15
SELLENGER'S ROUND-24
SEVEN STARS-10
SHE WANTS A FELLOW-11
SHEPTON MALLET HORNPIPE-54
SHIPDAM HORNPIPE-44
SIR SIDNEY SMITH'S MARCH-52
SLOE-55
SMITH'S A GALLANT FIREMAN-3
SOLDIERS JOY-6
SPEED THE PLOUGH-47
SPEED THE PLOUGH-49
SPIRIT OF THE DANCE-15
SPORTSMAN'S HORNPIPE-47
STATEN ISLAND-49
STEAM BOAT-45
STINGO-25
STRINGERS HORNPIPE-39
SWEEP'S POLKA-55
SWISS BOY-46
SWORD KNOT-39

T

TANK-41
TANKARD OF ALE-65
TATTER JACK WALSH-69
THREE AROUND THREE-33
TIP TOP POLKA NO.1-34
TIP TOP POLKA NO.2-34
TOM MELLINS HP-64
TRIP TO CARTMELL-1
TRIUMPH-46
TRUMPET HORNPIPE-40

U

UNCLE BERNARD'S-57
UNCLE GEORGES-2
UNCLE JIM'S-9
UNCLE'S JIG-16
UPTON-ON-SEVERN-67

W

WAITING FOR THE FEDERALS-6
WALTER BULWARS-53
WHIM-26
WHINHAM'S REEL-61
WHITEFRIAR'S HORNPIPE-26
WILTSHIRE SIX HAND REEL-35
WINSTER GALLOP-53
WONDER HORNPIPE-41
WOODLAND FLOWERS-67

WORCESTER HORNPIPE-42

BEWICK'S HORNPIPE
ROBERT BEWICK, 1797-1849

MORPETH RANT

Help the Cutty Sark Rise Again

Sea Shanties and Naval Hornpipes
at the Lord Hood Public House.

THE ROGUES' MARCH

COCK O' THE NORTH

THE DRESSED SHIP

THE BEAR DANCE

MAJOR MALLEY'S REEL

GILDEROY

JACKY TAR

SELLENGERS ROUND

PICKING OF STICKS

THE OLD MOLE

JACKS GONE A-SHEARING

PUNCHENELLO'S HORNPIPE, OR THE THREE RUSTY SWORDS

THE DUSTY MILLER

THE KEYS TO THE CELLAR

JOCKEY SAID TO JENNY

THE RUSSIAN WALTZ
THOMAS HARDY (I THINK)

THE BARNACLE WALTZ

36

GYPSEY'S HORNPIPE

THE DORSETSHIRE HORNPIPE

THE INSCRUTABLE TERRIER OF BELSTONE   W. ANDREWS © WREN TRUST 1998

THE LONDON HORNPIPE

SCHOTTISCHE HORNPIPE

BOB CANN

THE GLOUCESTER HORNPIPE

KAFOOLZALUM

THE KEEL ROW

SIR SIDNEY SMITH'S MARCH
ATTRIB. JAMES HOOK

NAPOLEON'S GRAND MARCH

54

DORSET FOUR HAND REEL

BUTTERED PEAS

SHEPTON MALLET HORNPIPE

OLD LANCASHIRE HORNPIPE

A TANKARD OF ALE

LILLI BURLERO

JIG OF SLURS

ATHOL HIGHLANDER